THE PRINCIPLE OF INVESTING FOR YOUR FUTURE

How to invest in your future and avoid costly mistakes.

RAFAEL JOHNSON

THE PRINCIPLE OF INVESTING FOR YOUR FUTURE.

Chapter 1: Decide on whether you will be an investor or a spender.

Chapter 2: You must learn to avoid an all-consuming lifestyle.

Chapter 3: The Investment Principles Work One Step at a Time.

Chapter 4: You must invest in yourself.

Chapter 5: Adaptable Investment Strategy

Chapter 6: Examine, research and investigate financial opportunities.

Chapter 7: Pay off your debts.

Chapter 8: Continually look for ways to increase and add value to what you do.

Chapter 9: Once you begin to put your money away, resolve never to touch it.

Chapter 10: Don't ever give up.

Chapter 1: Decide on whether you will be an investor or a spender.

Saving money as you can is an excellent approach to prepare for the unexpected and move closer to larger financial objectives like retirement. The two methods most individuals use to do this are investing or saving.

You likely comprehend how saving operates. But how exactly does investing operate, and how do you choose your investments?

No one has ever been successful in a significant way without making an investment. J. Paul Getty, the richest man in the world at the time, famously penned the line, "I have an allergy." My allergy to spending money has been present since I was a small child.

What did you do today to advance your company first? Have you met for coffee with a potential client or written the market letter quarterly? Was it a client financial plan review or an interview with a possible new hire? How are things going for the rest of the day? Will your focus be on advancing the company toward your vision or merely ensuring that it survives another day?

As a person who works in finance, you are aware that making an investment in the future has the potential to yield far bigger returns than making purchases today. Do you spend money or do you invest it in the future when you conduct business?

You need to have an idea of what your business will become before you can invest in it. It is the same procedure used when building clients' investment portfolios or financial plans. You must learn what your client wants for the future, whether it be funding for retirement, tuition costs, beginning a business, or a future wealth transfer. The actions that must be taken now, tomorrow, and so on are determined by specifying a future consequence. For the purpose of future results, a client makes an investment.

Without a future strategy or vision, a client is considerably more likely to spend than to invest. Isn't it more enjoyable to enjoy the immediate gratification of a new home, car, wardrobe, or vacation than to say, "I'll save this for later"? Spending is frequently the default option if there is no compelling future vision.

Apply this analogy to your company. Without a vision, you may waste time on endeavors that won't add anything to the future. One frequent marketing activity for you can be frequent networking at your local chamber of commerce. However, if your ideal client—the individual most likely to gain from your vision—is not present, you have simply spent time rather than invested it. It is unlikely that you genuinely know who your ideal client is and where to find them if you don't have a vision for your company and who it serves. You are making a purchase because you want to cross marketing off your list of things to accomplish.

Visionary financial advisors are aware of the activities that will advance their preparation for the future. They can network with other businesspeople who share their principles by serving on the board of a non-profit organization. Deeper connections are forged, recommendations are given, and a larger, more significant network is developed.

Spend some time crafting your vision. If you invest in your team with a vision, you will collectively find a variety of methods to grow that investment and reap a variety of rewards along the way.

Chapter 2: You must learn to avoid an all-consuming lifestyle.

Many individuals throughout history and the present have chosen to live a minimalist lifestyle that opposes and defeats materialism. Discover inspiration in their example. And you acknowledge that you can join their ranks. Every victory starts there.

You'll be led to believe in our world that the money you spend is what you give back to society the most. Every day, several advertisements beg for us to make additional purchases. As a result, each household's average consumer debt is quite high; there are more malls than high schools; Americans spend more money on jewelry and shoes than on higher education; and 93% of adolescent females say that shopping is their favorite leisure time. Although acknowledging your own consumeristic perspective won't immediately free you from it, it is a crucial first step.

"Comparison is the thief of joy," said Theodore Roosevelt once. Naturally, he was entirely correct. We lose happiness, joy, and fulfillment as soon as we start comparing our lives and things to those around us who have more. And we should start working hard to narrow the deficit. This is due to the fact that we constantly look upward, towards people who have more. However, if we began to pay more attention to those who lack, spend more time with those who have less, and choose to be happy in our circumstances, we might be able to begin to escape the consumerism-trap.

The financial resources we have earned or received also have a lot of potential. They can be utilized to support the less fortunate. They can be employed to offer justice and hope to a world in need of both. Furthermore, we should have higher aspirations for our money than just shopping on a department store's sale rack.

Every day, we are bombarded with advertisements on nearly every flat surface we encounter. It is a daily struggle to resist and defeat consumerism. Expect it to be that way. And renew your commitment each morning—or, if necessary, every hour. To exist is to consume, yet we were made for much larger things.

We will reach our full potential more quickly if we free ourselves from overconsumption. Stay away from the consumer generation. Imagine your future; in reality, you are laying the groundwork for freedom in the future. Investing would be that.

Chapter 3: The Investment Principles Work One Step at a Time.

When you invest money, you don't do it to get rich soon. You need to develop a longer-range perspective when you consider.

The best investors did not become famous overnight. It takes time, patience, trial, and error, as well as learning about yourself as an investor, to understand the ins and outs of the financial world.

You must prepare for successful investing as though you were embarking on a lengthy journey rather than a single event. Plan your investing route after first determining your destination. Are you, for instance, 55 years old and hoping to retire in 20 years? How much money are you going to need for this? You must start by asking these questions. Your investment objectives will determine the strategy you develop.

You are the best person to understand yourself and your circumstances. Because of this, you might be the most competent person to handle your own investments; all you need is a little assistance. Decide which aspects of your personality will help or hurt your ability to invest profitably and handle them accordingly.

Fund managers created a behavioral model that is incredibly helpful for helping investors understand themselves. Be wary of faux allies, such as dishonest investment advisers, whose objectives can be at odds with your own. Also keep in mind that, as an investor, you are up against powerful institutions of finance with access to more resources, including knowledge, more quickly.

Always keep in mind that you could be your own worst adversary. You could be undermining your own success, depending on your personality, strategy, and unique situation. A guardian would be acting against their personality type if they tried to make quick money by following the most recent market fad. You would be far more impacted by significant losses that can be a result of high-risk, high-return investments because you are risk averse and value asset preservation. Recognize and address the obstacles keeping you from making profitable investments or stepping beyond your comfort zone by being honest with yourself.

Chapter 4: You must invest in yourself.

Your self-esteem will increase and your confidence in your skills will grow as a result of investing in yourself. Focusing on your personal development will help you learn new information and abilities, as well as better understand yourself.

The best investment you ever make might be in yourself by learning to invest in yourself. It produces not only future benefits but also, frequently, an immediate pay-off. The most crucial investment you can make for your financial future is in your own development, whether it is in information or abilities. To broaden your knowledge and keep up with the times, this entails making educational investments.

The most crucial investment you can make is in yourself, regardless of what other investments you make, including paper assets (such as stocks and bonds), commodities, real estate, owning businesses, or even your time at work. Your investments in these vehicles may lose value as the economy changes in today's unstable globe.

In addition, if your abilities deteriorate and become outmoded, you risk losing your marketability, employability, or competitive advantage. You are the center of your money, regardless of where it comes from.

Putting emphasis on investing in both personal and professional growth is the surest way to improve life quality and be successful, productive, and fulfilled. The amount of work you put into constantly investing in yourself will determine how well your life turns out, both now and in the future.

Even if it's a possibility and, depending on your employment field, perhaps a necessity, investing in higher education isn't always the best way to advance your abilities. You can make a variety of investments in your knowledge and abilities.

A smart investor spreads his sources of income. As a result, invest in yourself by learning new skills to keep your mind active, cultivating creative thinking, or starting a side business to make money. Examine your spending habits as well as your expenses. Spending money on items you can't afford or don't really need is a bad idea.

Additionally, increasing your level of knowledge and expertise isn't just restricted to the corporate world and doesn't always have to be formal. Numerous opportunities exist for "skill investment."

You should put your money into things that have generated income for you. Prior to entering the stock market, concentrate your investment "first" on the industry you can affect. Invest in your own labor of love and ambition.

Chapter 5: Adaptable Investment Strategy

Your funds are invested in the places you decide, and the funds you choose are purchased with your assets. Different funds make investments in various kinds of assets. Some investors, for instance, only invest in real estate, while others buy stocks directly, and still others invest in a variety of assets.

Before you retire personally, you can start doing this. Spend between 10% and 15% of your income on insurance.

Chapter 6: Examine, research and investigate financial opportunities.

Don't invest your money right away. If something seems too good to be true, it most likely is. Stay away from "get rich quick" schemes of any kind.

The path you take should depend on your level of education, personality, and resources. Typically, investors choose one of the following approaches:

- Avoid placing all your eggs in one basket. Diversify, in other words.
- Don't put all of your eggs in one basket, and keep an eye on it.

By placing tactical bets on a main passive portfolio, you can combine these two approaches.

Most successful investors begin with diverse, low-risk portfolios and progressively pick up skills via experience. Investors that get more knowledgeable over time are better suited to managing their investments more actively.

Although, it is difficult to foresee the market, one thing is certain: it will be volatile. Being a successful investor requires steady learning, and the investment process is frequently drawn out. You may occasionally be proven wrong by the market. Recognize this and learn from your mistakes.

Chapter 7: Pay off your debts.

For the remainder of your life, refrain from taking on debt. People with little or no debt tend to amass large sums of money over the course of their lives. The first step is to never buy something that you cannot afford.

Decide to stop carrying debt straight away. That implies you can stop using your credit card. No more obtaining personal loans to pay for items you can't afford in cash. Has a nerve been touched yet? This may represent a substantial shift in pace for some of you. The only way to truly change your life, though, is to quit doing what you've always done and make room for something new. Your life can only be changed by you, but you don't have to do it by yourself.

You can watch the majority of your favorite shows online in this age, so welcome. Cut the cord now if you haven't already! Watch how rapidly your debt snowball begins to grow as you apply that $100 cable bill toward your debt each month. You should sell all the items you wasted money on and use the proceeds to settle your debts.

Additionally, you should stop paying for any memberships that do so on a recurring basis to see how your life improves.

Chapter 8: Continually look for ways to increase and add value to what you do.

The simplest method to add value is to speed up the rate at which you provide the kind of value that customers are ready to pay for.

Successful people understand that everyone is impatient. Someone who didn't know they needed your product or service until today now needs it urgently. People believe that speed and the value of your offering are directly correlated.

Someone who can complete the task quickly for you is regarded as more capable and as providing a higher level of quality than someone who completes the task slowly or whenever they get around to it.

The second secret to building money is offering superior quality to your rivals at the same price.

Not to mention, quality is defined by what the client says it is. Finding out what your customer wants and offering it to them faster than your competition is the finest definition of total quality management.

Quality encompasses more than just increased durability or superior design. Utility, or the use to which the client must put the product or service, is the first thing that is meant by quality. In the eyes of the consumer, quality is determined by his or her individual demand or desired benefit.

These product or service characteristics become the bare minimum, or the accepted standard, in the market if everyone is providing the same thing.

If you want to stand out as a person or a producer, you must "plus" what you are doing in order for your client to view you and your product as being better than those of your rivals.

A product or service can gain value by having better packaging or design. By streamlining its usage, you can raise its value. By making computers simple to use for the average individual, Apple revolutionized the whole computer industry. For Apple and the countless other businesses that have taken the same path, simplicity has grown to be a huge source of additional value.

Since individuals are primarily emotional beings, enhancing customer service is another way to add value and increase wealth.

They are significantly impacted by customer service agents' warmth, friendliness, joy, and assistance. In a market that is changing quickly, many businesses are relying heavily on their superior customer service. Discounts at certain intervals can help you grow your company and enhance the quality of your job.

Adding value of some kind is the source of all wealth. Give your clients more worth. At work, go above and above.

Chapter 9: Once you begin to put your money away, resolve never to touch it.

Financial freedom is the primary motivation for saving money, but the truth is that saving money extends beyond simply stashing some cash for emergencies.

You need to be wise with your money since what you do with it greatly affects how much of a difference you can make.

Don't ever do these things to your savings;

- Spending it

Savings withdrawals can be highly alluring, especially when you're short on money. Set a savings goal and make a commitment to yourself not to touch it until you've reached it.

- Lend it out.

Never lend family members or friends money that you have saved up. Savings cannot be lent out, but money from another source can. Loaning money from your savings is not a wise decision because you cannot be sure that the other party will pay back the loan.

- Unplanned expenditure

Never put money into a venture you are unfamiliar with. Do some research and educate yourself before deciding to invest. You didn't put money aside to gamble with. Consider your risks carefully, avoid becoming overly greedy, and start looking for ways to double your money.

- Disseminate it

Before you choose to be kind to everyone and follow the path of philanthropy, you need to be financially independent. Prior to making a social contribution, first focus on increasing your money.

- Delay saving it in an account for so long.

Given that you can use it, why keep your money in your account? Saving money is a good thing, but keeping it in a savings account for too long without doing anything with it is not the best. Once you have enough, look for profitable activities you can engage in with your savings. In a few years, the real value of money will have decreased due to rising costs.

No matter what happens, except to create your own "financial fortress."

Chapter 10: Don't ever give up.

Building money is a gradual process that leads to financial independence. It takes a great deal of perseverance and consistency to work, save, and invest month after month after year for a decade or perhaps three decades. According to the Bible, "steady progress leads to prosperity whereas rash conjecture leads to poverty."

www.ingramcontent.com/pod-product-compliance
Lightning Source LLC
LaVergne TN
LVHW052115160826
845678LV00015B/3562